Travel Guide for Your 40-Day Journey to A More Generous Life

Week 1

Week 2

Week 3

Week 4

Week 5

Week 6

Dear Fellow Shipmate:

Welcome aboard!

You are about to embark on a journey to a brave new world—a world of experiencing God in life-changing ways. It is not a world of buying and keeping, but of receiving and sharing, a world not focused on fleeting pleasures and momentary happiness, but discovering true contentment and everlasting joy.

To make this journey more meaningful and memorable, I invite you to take this journey with others. This trip is designed to be an all-hands-on-deck experience. Be sure to include any family members, friends, Bible study group, or people from church with you on this journey since what you discover will change all of your lives forever!

When our family went through this booklet, we went through the daily readings and financial quotes together. Each day we prayed about what God was teaching us. We talked about the results from the weekly projects. We discussed some of the weekly questions in our family and also with a group at church. All of us were impacted by this life-changing journey in positive ways.

So, by invitation of the King of Kings, I welcome you aboard on one of the most adventurous and thrilling journeys you'll ever experience—a journey to a more generous life.

I look forward to seeing you on the far shore!

Brian Kluth
Pastor and Founder of www.MAXIMUMgenerosity.org

Week 1

Just tell me what to do and I will do it, Lord. As long as I live I'll whole-heartedly obey. Make me walk along the right paths, for I know how delightful they really are.^{TLB}

Psalm 119:33-35

DAY 1
God is the Owner of everything.
(including all that you currently have or ever will have)

Think about, discuss or pray about the verse that relates most to your life

Psalm 50:10-12 (God says) "Every animal of the forest is mine, and the cattle on a thousand hills…and the creatures of the field are mine…the world is mine, and all that is in it."

Haggai 2:8 " The silver is mine and the gold is mine," declares the LORD Almighty.

1 Chronicles 29:11-12 "Everything in heaven and earth is yours (O Lord)…Wealth and honor come from you; you are the ruler of all things."

Leviticus 25:23 (God says) "The land is mine and you are but aliens and my tenants."

1 Chronicles 29:14-16 (David's prayer after people gave generously to a building project) "But who am I, and who are my people, that we should be able to give as generously as this? Everything comes from you, and we have given you only what comes from your hand. We are aliens and strangers in your sight, as were all our forefathers. Our days on earth are like a shadow, without hope. O LORD our God, as for all this abundance that we have provided for building you a temple for your Holy Name, it comes from your hand, and all of it belongs to you."

Psalm 24:1 The earth is the LORD's, and everything in it, the world, and all who live in it.

If we belong to Christ, it's logical that everything we have truly belongs to Him. When we give to God, we are just taking our hands off what already belongs to Him.

DAY 2
God is the provider of every good thing in your life.

Think about, discuss or pray about the verse that relates most to your life.

James 1:17 Every good and perfect gift is from above, coming down from the Father of the heavenly lights.

Ephesians 1:3-4 Praise be to the God and Father of our Lord Jesus Christ, who has blessed us in the heavenly realms with every spiritual blessing in Christ.

Matthew 7:11-12 If you, then, though you are evil, know how to give good gifts to your children, how much more will your Father in heaven give good gifts to those who ask him!

2 Chronicles 1:11-12 Since you [Solomon] have not asked for a long life but for wisdom and knowledge to govern my people over whom I have made you king, therefore wisdom and knowledge will be given you. And I [the LORD] will also give you wealth, riches and honor.

Proverbs 8:18-22 (God says) "Unending riches, honor, justice, and righteousness are mine to distribute. My gifts are better than the purest gold or sterling silver! Those who love and follow me are indeed wealthy. I fill their treasuries." TLB

Isaiah 26:12 All that we have accomplished you [Oh LORD] have done for us.

As thunder follows lightning, giving follows grace. When God's grace touches you, you can't help but respond with generous giving. Randy Alcorn

Give to God what's right—not what's left.

Practical Advice about Giving

By Brian Kluth, Pastor and Founder of www.MAXIMUMgenerosity.org

Here is some practical advice for people who have questions, doubts or fears about giving to the Lord's work.

If you are NOT a Christian: Don't worry about giving to God. Instead, realize and accept what God wants to give to you – complete forgiveness, a brand new start, the power to be good and to do good for others, help for your problems, the ability to forgive, and a home in heaven. If you recognize your need for these things, pray and invite Jesus Christ to bring these things into your life.

For all Christians: Always make it a priority to faithfully support the work of your local church first. Then give special gifts and offerings to other Christian causes, projects, missions or the needy as God leads you.

If you're fearful about giving 10% or more of your income to the Lord, try a 90-day test: In Malachi 3:10 God invites people to "test Him" in the matter of tithing (giving the first 10% of your income to God's work). Therefore, I encourage people to try a 90-day test. Begin giving 10% of your income to the Lord's work and watch and see if God does not begin working in your life in ways you haven't previously experienced. If you regret that decision OR if you feel you never experienced God's divine help in your finances during this time period, then discontinue the test. However, if you experience God's help, joyfully continue giving 10% or more to the Lord's work.

If you want to begin to actively give to God FIRST: Here are four different ideas to choose from:

1) Whenever you get any money, set aside 10% or more to give as the Lord directs.
2) Whenever you put a deposit in your checkbook, write out the first check(s) to God's work for 10% or more.
3) If you track your finances through a bookkeeping system or computer program, set up a category for church giving and another one for other Christian causes. Then begin to faithfully set aside 10% or more of your income into these accounts.

9

4) If you like to handle your finances electronically, consider using www.networkforgood.org or the electronic giving option from your church (if available) to faithfully give 10% or more to the Lord.

If you are married to a Christian, but the two of you do not agree on how much you should give to the Lord's work: See if your spouse will read through this material and/or listen to some of the internet messages at www.MAXIMUMgenerosity.org. Then talk and pray together about a mutually agreeable "testing period" concerning your giving 10% or more.

If you are married and your spouse is not a Christian: Identify any money you have freedom to spend (read Luke 8:3) and set aside 10% or more of this money to give to the Lord's work AND/OR show this material to your spouse and see if you can try the 90-day testing period.

If you are deciding whether to give off the gross or the net of your income: Pray and ask God what He wants you to do. If He prompts you in your heart to give off the gross amount, go ahead and do this, trusting Him with the results. If you don't have a peace about this, begin giving 10% off the net amount for a few months and see what happens. After a few months, if you experience God's creative care in your life, then begin to give 10% or more off of your gross income.

If you're wondering about how much to give to your church and how much to give to other places: A good practice I have used is to give 10% of my main source of income to my local church (i.e. my main income goes to support the work of my main source of Christian fellowship and teaching). Then, I use 10% or more of all other incomes sources and unexpected blessings to help fund other Christian needs and opportunities that God brings into my life.

If you have children at home: Help your children set up a place where they can set aside "God's portion" of any money they receive (i.e., allowances, work projects, gifts of money, etc.). Have them give at church, to missions, and/or to help people in need.

If you have "fallen behind" in your giving to God's work: If you knowingly or accidentally have fallen behind in your giving to God's work, you will never regret the decision to "get right" in this area. Review your financial records from the past several months and pray about "making up" the amount you have fallen behind. One elderly lady in her 90's I heard about sent a tithe check to the church office with the note, "I want to be prayed up, paid up, and ready to go!"

DAY 3

Your role is to be the trustee, manager and steward of 100% of what God entrusts to you during your lifetime.

Think about, discuss or pray about the verse that relates most to your life:

Colossians 3:17, 23-24 Whatever you do or say, let it be as a representative of the Lord Jesus....Whatever you do, work at it with all your heart, as working for the Lord, not for men, since you know that you will receive an inheritance from the Lord as a reward. It is the Lord Christ you are serving. TLB

Romans 14:7-8 None of us lives to himself alone and none of us dies to himself alone. If we live, we live to the Lord; and if we die, we die to the Lord.

Matthew 25:19-21, 24-26 "After a long time their master returned from his trip and called them to give an account of how they had used his money. The servant to whom he had entrusted the five bags of gold said, 'Sir, you gave me five bags of gold to invest, and I have doubled the amount.' The master was full of praise. 'Well done, my good and faithful servant. You have been faithful in handling this small amount, so now I will give you many more responsibilities. Let's celebrate together!'... "Then the servant with the one bag of gold came and said, 'Sir, I know you are a hard man, harvesting crops you didn't plant and gathering crops you didn't cultivate. I was afraid I would lose your money, so I hid it in the earth and here it is.' "But the master replied, 'You wicked and lazy servant!" NLT

1 Corinthians 4:2 It is required in stewards that a man be found faithful. KJV

Martin Luther said, "People go through 3 conversions: The conversion of their head, their heart and their pocketbook. Unfortunately, not all at the same time." Have you gone through all 3 conversions?

DAY 4
The LORD watches your giving.

Think about, discuss or pray about the verse that relates most to your life:

Mark 12:41-44 Jesus sat down opposite the place where the offerings were put and watched the crowd putting their money into the temple treasury. Many rich people threw in large amounts.
But a poor widow came and put in two very small copper coins, worth only a fraction of a penny. Calling his disciples to him, Jesus said, "I tell you the truth, this poor widow has put more into the treasury than all the others. They all gave out of their wealth; but she, out of her poverty, put in everything– all she had to live on."

Luke 21:1 Jesus saw the rich putting their gifts into the temple treasury.

2 Corinthians 8:12 For if the willingness is there, the gift is acceptable according to what one has, not according to what he does not have.

Exodus 35:22,27,29 All who were willing, men and women alike, came and brought gold jewelry of all kinds: brooches, earrings, rings and ornaments. They all presented their gold as a wave offering to the LORD…The leaders brought onyx stones and other gems…
All the Israelite men and women who were willing brought to the LORD freewill offerings for all the work the LORD through Moses had commanded them to do.

2 Chronicles 24:10-11 All the officials and all the people brought their contributions gladly, dropping them into the chest until it was full.

Your bank and credit card statements are theological documents. They tell who and what you worship.

With the price of everything else going up these days, aren't you glad the Lord hasn't increased the tithe to 15%?

DAY 5
Don't become prideful about anything God has entrusted to you.

Think about, discuss or pray about the verse that relates most to your life:

Deuteronomy 8:17-18 You may say to yourself, "My power and the strength of my hands have produced this wealth for me." But remember the LORD your God, for it is he who gives you the ability to produce wealth.

Psalm 62:10 If your riches increase, don't be proud.

Deuteronomy 8:11-14 Be careful that you do not forget the LORD your God… Otherwise, when you eat and are satisfied, when you build fine houses and settle down, and when your herds and flocks grow large and your silver and gold increase and all you have is multiplied, then your heart will become proud and you will forget the LORD your God.

Jeremiah 9:23-24 The Lord says, "Let not the…rich man boast of his riches, but let him who boasts boast about this: that he understands and knows Me."

Psalm 39:5-6 Proud man! Frail as breath! A shadow! And all his busy rushing ends in nothing. He heaps up riches for someone else to spend. ᵀᴸᴮ

Mark 8:36 What good is it for a man to gain the whole world, yet forfeit his soul?

Proverbs 16:19 Better to be poor and humble than proud and rich. ᵀᴸᴮ

Obadiah 1:3-7 "The pride of your heart has deceived you, you who… make your home on the heights, you who say to yourself, 'Who can bring me down to the ground?' Though you soar like the eagle and make your nest among the stars, from there I will bring you down," declares the LORD… "Oh, what a disaster awaits you…Your friends will deceive and overpower you."

When a man becomes rich, either God gains a partner or the man loses his soul.

DAY 6
Even the poor are to give to God from what they have.

Think about, discuss or pray about the verse that relates most to your life:

Deuteronomy 16:16 No man should appear before the LORD empty-handed.

1 Kings 17:10-15 (Elijah asked a widow) "Would you please bring me a cup of water?" As she was going to get it, he called to her, "Bring me a bite of bread, too." But she said, "I swear by the LORD your God that I don't have a single piece of bread in the house. And I have only a handful of flour left in the jar and a little cooking oil in the bottom of the jug. I was just gathering a few sticks to cook this last meal, and then my son and I will die." But Elijah said to her, "Don't be afraid! Go ahead and cook that `last meal,' but bake me a little loaf of bread first. Afterward there will still be enough food for you and your son. For this is what the LORD, the God of Israel, says: There will always be plenty of flour and oil left in your containers until the time when the LORD sends rain and the crops grow again!" So she did as Elijah said, and she and Elijah and her son continued to eat from her supply of flour and oil for many days. For no matter how much they used, there was always enough left in the containers, just as the LORD had promised through Elijah. NLT

Genesis 28:20-22 (While a single young man with no job or income) Jacob made a vow, saying, "If God will be with me and will watch over me… then the LORD will be my God…and of all that you (O God) give me I will give you a tenth."

2 Corinthians 8:2-4 Though (the Macedonian Christians) have been going through much trouble and hard times, they have mixed their wonderful joy with their deep poverty, and the result has been an overflow of giving to others. They gave not only what they could afford but far more; and I can testify that they did it because they wanted to…They begged us to take the money so they could share in the joy of helping the Christians in Jerusalem. TLB

If a pauper gives to God, he'll feel like a prince.
If a prince doesn't give to God,
he'll feel like a pauper.

DAY 7

Set up a plan to faithfully give 10% OR MORE of your financial resources to the Lord's work.

Think about, discuss or pray about the verse that relates most to your life:

Luke 11:42 (Jesus said) "Though you are careful to tithe even the smallest part of your income, you completely forget about justice and the love of God. You should tithe, yes, but you should not leave these other things undone." ᵀᴸᴮ

Deuteronomy 14:22,23 Be sure to set aside a tenth of all that your fields produce…The purpose of tithing is to teach you always to put God first in your lives. ᵀᴸᴮ

Exodus 22:29 You must be prompt in giving Me the tithe…

Genesis 14:20 Abram gave…a tenth of everything.

Malachi 3:8-11 "Will a man rob God? Surely not! And yet you have robbed me. '"What do you mean? When did we ever rob you?' "You have robbed me of the tithes and offerings due to me. And so the awesome curse of God is cursing you…Bring all the tithes into the storehouse so that there will be food enough in my Temple; if you do, I will open up the windows of heaven for you and pour out a blessing so great you won't have room enough to take it in! "Try it! Let me prove it to you! Your crops will be large, for I will guard them from insects and plagues. Your grapes won't shrivel away before they ripen," says the Lord Almighty. ᵀᴸᴮ

2 Chronicles 31:5,12 The people responded immediately and generously with the first of their crops and grain, new wine, olive oil, money, and everything else – a tithe of all they owned. They faithfully brought in the contributions, tithes and dedicated gifts. ᵀᴸᴮ

Giving 10% isn't the ceiling of giving; it's the floor. It's not the finish line of giving; it's just the starting blocks.

THE FAITHFUL GIVER'S 7 GREAT SURPRISES...

When you begin to actively and faithfully return 10% or more of all your income to the Lord's work, you will be surprised at...

1. The generous amount of money you will be able to give to the Lord's work.

2. The deepening of your spiritual life through trusting the Lord to meet your needs.

3. The increased ease in which you meet your other financial obligations on the 9/10th's of the income you have left.

4. The way that starting to give 10% leads to more generous giving than you ever dreamed possible.

5. The effect faithful giving has in making you a wiser manager over all the rest of the money and possessions you have.

6. The unexpected provisions that God brings into your life.

7. And the surprise you have when you wish you had started giving 10% or more much sooner.

"I absolutely believe in the power of tithing. My own experience is that the more I give away, the more that comes back."

KEN BLANCHARD, AUTHOR OF THE "ONE MINUTE MANAGER"

IDENTIFY: "WHERE IS THE MONEY COMING FROM?"

"Honor the Lord by giving him the first part of all your income."
Proverbs 3:9

"The purpose of tithing (giving 10% of your income) is to teach you always to put God first in your lives."
Deuteronomy 14:23

Step 1 Check ☑ all items that are sources of God-given cash flow or income that you anticipate in your life during the next 12 months.

Step 2 Determine an approximate "financial value" ($ amount) for each item checked. Indicate the frequency of how often you receive these funds (W=Weekly, B=Bi-weekly or twice a month, M=Monthly, Q=Quarterly, Y=Yearly/annually, S=Sporadically or O=One-time amount).

Step 3 Indicate the amount (10% of the value) IF you were to honor the Lord with the first 10% of this God-given resource.

Step 4 Prayerfully review the list and circle any areas where you feel you should begin to faithfully give at least 10% to God's work.

Step 5 Prayerfully identify and star (*) any items you feel God is prompting you to dedicate a larger percentage (even up to 100%) to meet a special need or giving opportunity. Possibly this is income you are not counting on, do not actively need, or that could be given as a sacrificial offering.

☑	CASH & INCOME IN NEXT 12 MONTHS	VALUE/FREQ	IF 10% = $
☐	Income, wage or salary from:		
☐	Income, wage or salary from:		
☐	Income, wage or salary from:		
☐	Overtime pay		
☐	Bonuses		
☐	Tax returns/refunds		
☐	Commissions		
☐	Business income		
☐	Severance Pay		
☐	Part-time work or moonlighting		
☐	Consulting fees		
☐	Sale of products or assets		
☐	Home-based business or services		
☐	Sale of stuff I/we own		
☐	Social Security		
☐	Pension/Retirement accounts		
☐	Military or union pay		
☐	Annuity		
☐	Disability income		
☐	Unemployment or Workmen's Comp		
☐	Spousal or child support		
☐	Trust fund		
☐	Inheritance monies		
☐	Insurance settlement		
☐	Legal settlement		
☐	Income from rental or leased properties		
☐	Interest and /or Dividends		
☐	Repayment of personal loans		
☐	Royalties from copyrights/patents		
☐	Rebates/Refunds/Returns/Coupons		
☐	Government welfare, food stamps, etc.		
☐	Other:		
☐	Other:		
☐	Other:		
	CHILDREN		
☐	Work projects		
☐	Allowances		
☐	Cash gifts (b-day, Christmas, etc.)		
☐	Part-time jobs or home business		
☐	Babysitting, lawn mowing, etc.		
☐	Other:		

Week 1
SHARING YOUR TREASURES

1. As a child, what was one of your earliest or most vivid recollections about giving money to God OR what do you recall about your parent's practices and attitudes about giving to God?

2. When you filled out the worksheet for the first week's project, "Income", what surprised you or caught your attention in doing this exercise?

3. What truth or Bible verse from the past seven days of reading stood out to you the most?

4. Who is the most financially generous person you know?

5. How old were you when the idea of tithing (giving 10% of your income) came into your conscious thoughts?

6. If you do not faithfully give 10% or more of your income to the Lord's work, what do you think are the real reasons you're holding back from doing this?

7. If you do faithfully give 10% or more of your income to the Lord's work, how old were you and what were the financial circumstances in your life when you first started tithing?

8. If you do faithfully give 10% or more of your income to the Lord's work, what are the values and benefits you've seen by faithfully doing this?

9. What do you feel is the difference between giving tithes and giving offerings?

10. How do you make sure that giving to your local church is the first priority in your Christian giving?

Week 2

Your word is a lamp to my feet and a light for my path.

Psalm 119:105

DAY 8
Don't trust in your riches, but trust in God.

Think about, discuss or pray about the verse that relates most to your life:

Proverbs 11:28 Whoever trusts in his riches will fall, but the righteous will thrive like a green leaf.

1 Timothy 6:17 Command those who are rich in this present world not to be arrogant nor to put their hope in wealth, which is so uncertain, but to put their hope in God.

John 14:1 Do not let your hearts be troubled. Trust in God.

Job 31:24-28 (Job said) "If I have put my trust in gold or said to pure gold, 'You are my security,' if I have rejoiced over my great wealth, the fortune my hands had gained...so that my heart was secretly enticed...then these also would be sins to be judged, for I would have been unfaithful to God on high."

Psalm 49:6-12 (Sinners) trust in their wealth and boast of great riches. Yet they cannot redeem themselves from death by paying a ransom to God. Redemption does not come so easily, for no one can ever pay enough to live forever and never see the grave. Those who are wise must finally die, just like the foolish and senseless, leaving all their wealth behind. The grave is their eternal home, where they will stay forever. They may name their estates after themselves, but they leave their wealth to others. They will not last long despite their riches—they will die like the animals. NLT

Are you rich?
Did you realize that if you personally make more than $1500 per year you are richer than 75% of the world's 6+ billion people!
To find out how your income compares to everyone else in the world go to: www.globalrichlist.com

DAY 9
Understand riches can deceive you.

Think about, discuss or pray about the verse that relates most to your life:

Revelation 3:17 "You say, 'I am rich, with everything I want; I don't need a thing!' And you don't realize that spiritually you are wretched and miserable and poor and blind and naked. ᵀᴸᴮ

Mark 8:36 What good is it for a man to gain the whole world, yet forfeit his soul?

Mark 4:18-19 Others, like seed sown among thorns, hear the word; but the worries of this life, the deceitfulness of wealth and the desires for other things come in and choke the word, making it unfruitful.

Luke 12:15 (Jesus said) "Watch out! Be on your guard against all kinds of greed; a man's life does not consist in the abundance of his possessions."

Proverbs 23:4-5 Don't weary yourself trying to get rich. Why waste your time? Riches can disappear as though they had the wings of a bird! ᵀᴸᴮ

Ecclesiastes 5:11 The more you have, the more you spend, right up to the limits of your income. So what is the advantage of wealth– except perhaps to watch it as it runs through your fingers! ᵀᴸᴮ

1 Timothy 6:10 The love of money is the first step toward all kinds of sin. Some people have even turned away from God because of their love for it, and as a result have pierced themselves with many sorrows. ᵀᴸᴮ

Galatians 6:7 If (a person) sows to please his own wrong desires, he will be planting seeds of evil and he will surely reap a harvest of spiritual decay and death. ᵀᴸᴮ

*The poorest man in the world
is the man who has nothing but money.*

Count Your Blessings

A pathway to more joyful and generous giving and living

A number of years ago, I discovered a wonderful verse in I Corinthians 16:2, "On the first day of each week let each of you lay something aside, storing up as he may prosper."

At first, I didn't understand how the verse could apply to my life. But my wife and I began a Sunday evening practice of "looking back and writing down" how God provided for us in the previous seven days. Each week, we discovered there were many ways that God provided for us outside of our normal income. We began giving 10% of my main income to our local church and we then started a "Blessings Fund" that represented 10% or more of the myriad of blessings God creatively brought into our life week by week.

At the end of the first year, even though my main income only brought in $15,000; I discovered we had given $1500 to our local church and an additional $2500 out of our "Blessings Fund" to other Christian causes. This meant that God had blessed us with $25,000 of blessings during the past year that was over and above my $15,000 salary!

We did this for several more years and discovered that each year God doubled and tripled what we were able and willing to give to the Lord's work because we counted our blessings. Here are the lessons we learned and practiced that helped us live a more joyful and generous life:

1. Plan a time each week where you will begin to write down God's provisions from the previous week in a "Blessings Notebook."

2. When you meet together, think back over the following areas and write down anything that comes to your remembrance:

   Main Income If you were paid during the week, write down that amount. For us, we gave 10% of this amount to our local church.

   Additional Income or Unexpected Cash: Write down any cash gifts, overtime pay, bonuses, second salary, moonlighting, investment returns, sale of any possession, refunds, inheritance, etc.

People's Hospitality? Meals, lodging, or entertainment that others gave to you or paid the cost.

Special Help or Assistance? Help with car, house, equipment repairs, free babysitting, etc.

Discount or Sale Items? Any money saved on discounted clothing or household items, garage sale/thrift shop savings, discounts on recreational activities, etc.

Purchase of New Possessions? When my wife and I were buying a major item or a luxury item, we sometimes included the cost of these items in our blessings fund in order to give an additional 10% or more to the Lord's work.

3. Write down the financial value for each item OR (very important) write down the amount you "WOULD HAVE BEEN WILLING TO SPEND" for the item. For example: A family member gave me a $1000 radial arm saw. I would have never been able or willing to afford a $1000 tool like this, but I might have "been willing to spend" $200 on a used radial arm saw at a garage sale. So, in this example, I put down the value of the blessing at $200 (not $1000). Therefore I ended up giving an extra $20 to the Lord's work, not an extra $100.

4. Add up the value of the total number of blessing items for the week and take 10% or more of the total and decide where to give it OR set aside the week's amount in your notebook or put the money in a special place or account and consider this your "BLESSINGS FUND".

5. Faithfully give your church 10% or more of your main income. Then begin to joyfully and generously use your "Blessings Fund" to help support missions, missionaries, special projects and needs, building programs, the needy, Christian workers and organizations.

4-Week Challenge:

I am confident that the LORD has been blessing most people's lives week by week. But most people don't "see" the blessings because they don't take time to "look back over the last seven days to see what God has done to provide for them." Because of this, I challenge you to try this for at least four weeks to see what God is doing for you! I believe it will truly lead you to a more joyful and generous life!

DAY 10
Train your children to be faithful and generous givers.

Think about, discuss or pray about the verse that relates most to your life:

Proverbs 22:6 Train up a child in the way he should go: and when he is old, he will not depart from it. KJV

Genesis 18:19 I have chosen him, so that he will direct his children and his household after him to keep the way of the LORD by doing what is right and just.

Deuteronomy 6:6-7 These commandments that I give you today are to be upon your hearts. Impress them on your children. Talk about them when you sit at home and when you walk along the road, when you lie down and when you get up.

Psalm 78:4-7 We will tell the next generation the praiseworthy deeds of the LORD, his power, and the wonders he has done. He decreed statutes…which he commanded our forefathers to teach their children, so the next generation would know them, even the children yet to be born, and they in turn would tell their children. Then they would put their trust in God and would not forget his deeds but would keep his commands.

Ephesians 6:4 Bring them (children) up with the loving discipline the Lord himself approves, with suggestions and godly advice. NLT

John D. Rockefeller said, "I never would have been able to tithe the first million dollars I ever made if I had not tithed on my first salary, which was $1.50 a week."

Giving a child money to put into an offering plate does not produce a generous adult. If you want to produce a generous adult, you must train a child to tithe from any money he or she receives from family, friends or work projects. This child will grow up to honor God.

DAY 11
Focus on being content with God's daily provisions.

Think about, discuss or pray about the verse that relates most to your life:

1 Timothy 6:6-8 Godliness with contentment is great gain. For we brought nothing into the world, and we can take nothing out of it. But if we have food and clothing, we will be content with that.

Ecclesiastes 5:10 Whoever loves money never has money enough; whoever loves wealth is never satisfied with his income.

Proverbs 30:8-9 Give me neither poverty nor riches! Give me just enough to satisfy my needs! For if I grow rich, I may become content without God. And if I am too poor, I may steal and thus insult God's holy name. NLT

Matthew 6:9-11 This is how you should pray: "'Our Father in heaven, hallowed be your name, your kingdom come, your will be done on earth as it is in heaven. Give us today our daily bread...'"

Philippians 4:11-13 I have learned to be content whatever the circumstances. I know what it is to be in need, & I know what it is to have plenty. I have learned the secret of being content in any and every situation, whether well fed or hungry, whether living in plenty or in want.

You are only poor when you want more than you have.

The trouble with most people is their earning capacity doesn't match their yearning capacity.

The most expensive vehicle to operate, per mile, is the shopping cart.

DAY 12

You cannot serve God "and" Money but you must learn to serve God "with" money.

Think about, discuss or pray about the verse that relates most to your life:

Luke 16:11-13 (Jesus said) "So if you have not been trustworthy in handling worldly wealth, who will trust you with true riches?…No servant can serve two masters. Either he will hate the one and love the other, or he will be devoted to the one and despise the other. You cannot serve both God and Money."

Proverbs 10:16 The good man's earnings advance the cause of righteousness. The evil man squanders his on sin.

Matthew 6:19-21 (Jesus said) "Do not store up for yourselves treasures on earth, where moth and rust destroy, and where thieves break in and steal. But store up for yourselves treasures in heaven, where moth and rust do not destroy, and where thieves do not break in and steal. For where your treasure is, there your heart will be also."

Proverbs 16:16 How much better to get wisdom than gold, to choose understanding rather than silver!

Proverbs 17:16 Of what use is money in the hand of a fool, since he has no desire to get wisdom?

1 Corinthians 4:2 It is required in stewards, that a man be found faithful. KJV

The world asks: "What does a person own?" God asks, "How is the person using what they have been given?"

A Christian is one who does not have to consult his bank book to see how wealthy he really is.

There are dangerous consequences
if you live for pleasure.

Think about, discuss or pray about the verse that relates most to your life:

Proverbs 21:17 He who loves pleasure will become poor.

Galatians 6:7 If a man sows to please his own wrong desires, he will be planting seeds of evil and he will surely reap a harvest of spiritual decay and death. ᵀᴸᴮ

Ecclesiastes 2:10-11 I denied myself nothing my eyes desired; I refused my heart no pleasure…Yet when I surveyed all that my hands had done and what I had toiled to achieve, everything was meaningless.

Ecclesiastes 7:4 A fool thinks only of having a good time now. ᵀᴸᴮ

2 Timothy 3:1-5 There will be terrible times in the last days. People will be lovers of themselves, lovers of money, …lovers of pleasure rather than lovers of God having a form of godliness but denying its power.

1 Timothy 5:6 The widow who lives for pleasure is dead even while she lives.

Proverbs 23:20-21 Don't carouse with drunkards and gluttons, for they are on their way to poverty. And remember that too much sleep clothes a man with rags. ᴺᴸᵀ

Luke 15:13 The younger son got together all he had, set off for a distant country and there squandered his wealth in wild living.

Your use of money shows what you think of God.

DAY 14
Don't live for this life,
but for your heavenly home.

Think about, discuss or pray about the verse that relates most to your life:

Luke 16:9 (Jesus said) "I tell you, use worldly wealth to gain friends for yourselves, so that when it is gone, you will be welcomed into eternal dwellings."

Hebrews 11:13-16 These men of faith…agreed that this earth was not their real home but that they were just strangers visiting down here…they were looking forward to their real home in heaven. If they had wanted to, they could have gone back to the good things of this world. But they didn't want to. They were living for heaven. And now God is not ashamed to be called their God, for he has made a heavenly city for them. ᵀᴸᴮ

Hebrews 13:14,16 For this world is not our home; we are looking forward to our everlasting home in heaven…Don't forget to do good and to share what you have. ᵀᴸᴮ

Hebrews 11:10 (Abraham) was looking forward to the city with foundations, whose architect and builder is God.

1 Corinthians 3:12-15 If any man builds on this foundation using gold, silver, costly stones, wood, hay or straw, his work will be shown for what it is, because the Day will bring it to light. It will be revealed with fire, and the fire will test the quality of each man's work. If what he has built survives, he will receive his reward. If it is burned up, he will suffer loss; he himself will be saved, but only as one escaping through the flames.

2 Corinthians 5:10 For we must all appear before the judgment seat of Christ, that each one may receive what is due him for the things done while in the body, whether good or bad.

Our real worth is what will be ours in eternity.

God's Desire
Is For Christians
To Learn To...

Give Cheerfully	2 Corinthians 9:7
Give Generously	2 Chronicles 31:5, 1 Chronicles 29:14-17, I Timothy 6:17-19
Give Systematically	Deuteronomy 14:22, Genesis 28:16-22, Proverbs 3:9-10
Give Reverently	Matthew 2:11, Deuteronomy 14:23, Leviticus 22:20, Malachi 1:6-9
Give Proportionally	1 Corinthians 16:2, Deuteronomy 16:17, Exodus 35:5, Ezra 2:69
Give Joyfully	2 Chronicles 24:10, 29:17, and 29:36, 2 Corinthians 8:2
Give Willingly	2 Corinthians 8:12, Exodus 35:21-22, 1 Chronicles 29:6
Give Regularly	Deuteronomy 16:16, 1 Corinthians 16:2, Nehemiah 10:35-39
Give Faithfully	Deuteronomy 14:27, 2 Chronicles 31:4-8
Give Expectantly	Malachi 3:8-10, Genesis 28:20-22, Luke 6:38, 2 Corinthians 9:6-11
Give Eternally	Matthew 6:19-20, 1 Timothy 6:19, Mark 10:21, Hebrews 11:13-16
Give Extravagantly	John 12:1-8, Mark 12:41-44, 1 Chronicles 29:2-9, Exodus 35
Give Thoughtfully	Haggai 1:3-11

IDENTIFY: "WHERE IS YOUR MONEY GOING?"

"Riches certainly make themselves wings;
They fly away like an eagle..." Proverbs 23:5

Money talks: It says, "good bye!" Where is your money going?

Step 1 As best as you can, estimate how much money you are spending on a "monthly basis" in each area listed on the next page (Helpful hint: Take ANY quarterly, yearly, sometimes and one-time expenses and prorate this amount on a monthly basis).

Step 2 Prayerfully review the list. Are there any items the Lord may be showing you that:
- You don't really need and could eliminate from your spending in order to be more generous?
- You could meet this need more affordably by shopping around or by lowering your expectations so you could be more generous?
- You should decrease or eliminate because you realize this expenditure is hurtful to your personal health OR your spiritual growth and service?
- You could postpone or trust God to meet this need in another way so that you could be more generous?

Step 3 Based on items you identified in step 2, determine any increased amount you could give to the Lord monthly to meet a special need or giving opportunity: $_____/month.

HELPFUL NOTE: If you would like to find out how your spending compares to recommended national budget averages, visit: www.crown.org and click on tools and their budget guide calculator.

WHERE IS YOUR MONEY GOING?

GIVING: Church: $_____   Building: $_____   Needy: $_____
Missions: $_____   Other: $_____   Other: $_____   Other: $_____

HOUSING: Rent/Mortgage: $_____   Utilities: $_____   Trash $_____
Lawn: $_____   Maintenance/Repairs: $_____   Furnishing/Decorations: $_____
Special Projects/Purchases: $_____   Other: $_____   Other: $_____

TELECOMMUNICATIONS: Phone: $_____   Long Distance: $_____
Cell Phone/s $_____   Internet: $_____   Other: $_____

VEHICLES: Payments: $_____   Gas: $_____   Insurance: $_____
Maint/Repair: $_____   License: $_____   Other: $_____

GROCERIES AND HOUSEHOLD: Groceries: $_____   Supplies: $_____
Miscellaneous: $_____

ENTERTAINMENT AND RECREATION: Health Club: $_____   Cable: $_____
Videos/Movies: $_____   Lessons: $_____   Crafts/Hobbies: $_____
Sports: $_____   Events/Concerts: $_____   Music: $_____   Vacations: $_____
Trips: $_____   Vacation Home: $_____   Camping: $_____
Hunting/Fishing: $_____   School/Scout/Civic Activities: $_____   Other: $_____
Alcohol*: $_____   Tobacco*: $_____   Gambling*: $_____
*These are not recommended uses, but rather are listed to help someone determine how much money they
may be spending unwisely on these items.

INSURANCES: Medical: $_____   Life: $_____   Disability: $_____   Other: $_____

CLOTHING: Man: $_____   Woman: $_____   Children: $_____

MISCELLANEOUS: Meals out at work: $_____   Childcare: $_____
Toiletries: $_____   Hair: $_____   Pets: $_____   Vet: $_____
Subscriptions: $_____   Other: $_____

GIFT GIVING & CELEBRATIONS: Anniversaries: $_____   Birthdays: $_____
Weddings/Babies/Grad: $_____   Holiday Parties: $_____   Other: $_____

MEDICAL: Doctors: $_____   Hospitals: $_____   Dental: $_____
Prescriptions: $_____   Therapy: $_____   Other: $_____

SAVINGS/INVESTMENTS: Savings: $_____   Pension: $_____   College: $_____
Investment: $_____   Other: $_____

EDUCATION: Tuition: $_____   Books: $_____   Fees/Activities: $_____
Room & Board: $_____   Other: $_____

DEBTS: Credit Card Payments: $_____   Personal Loans: $_____
Student Loans: $_____   Medical Bills: $_____   Other: $_____

Week 2
SHARING YOUR TREASURES

Possible questions to think about or discuss

1. What financial situation did you grow up with (i.e. not enough money, just made ends meets, more than enough, it varied, etc.)?

2. What did your parents do, if anything, to help train you to manage your finances?

3. What did you think about the "Count Your Blessings" article? Could this practice have any impact on your life and giving?

4. When you filled out the "Lifestyle" worksheet for this week's project, what surprised you or caught your attention in doing this exercise?

5. What was the most painful or difficult financial experience you ever recall going through?

6. Have you ever intentionally curtailed your normal spending in order to be more generous to the Lord's work? If so, when?

7. What truth or Bible verse from the past seven days of reading stood out to you the most?

8. What was the best financial advice or teaching you've ever received (from reading, seminars/conferences, personal example, or personal advice)?

9. What is one thing you spend your money on that is unhealthy for you or is a waste of money?

10. What is something you bought on impulse that you realized later you didn't really need?

11. If you began to experience tough times financially, would you try to take care of your own needs first or would you first make sure you first gave to God from whatever minimal resources you had available? Why?

Week 3

Help me to prefer obedience to making money! Turn me away from wanting any other plan than yours. Revive my heart toward you. Reassure me that your promises are for me, for I trust and revere you.[TLB]

Psalm 119:36-38

DAY 15
The desire for "more" can be a destructive force to your life and faith.

Think about, discuss or pray about the verse that relates most to your life:

1 Timothy 6:9-10 People who want to get rich fall into temptation and a trap and into many foolish and harmful desires that plunge men into ruin and destruction. For the love of money is a root of all kinds of evil. Some people, eager for money, have wandered from the faith and pierced themselves with many griefs.

Hebrews 13:5 Keep your lives free from the love of money and be content with what you have, because God has said, "Never will I leave you; never will I forsake you."

Ecclesiastes 5:10,12 Whoever loves money never has money enough; whoever loves wealth is never satisfied with his income…
The abundance of a rich man permits him no sleep.

Proverbs 20:17 Some men enjoy cheating, but the cake they buy with such ill-gotten gain will turn to gravel in their mouths.

Proverbs 20:21 Quick wealth is not a blessing in the end.

Habakkuk 2:9 How terrible it will be for you who get rich by unjust means!

Proverbs 11:24 It is possible to give freely and become more wealthy, but those who are stingy will lose everything.

It's not the high cost of living, it's the cost of living too high that gets most people in trouble.

When your outgo exceeds your income, your upkeep will lead to your downfall.

DAY 16

In building projects a large public gift and a group of leadership gifts can glorify God and result in great generosity and rejoicing.

Think about, discuss or pray about the verse that relates most to your life:

1 Chronicles 29:1-9 Then King David turned to the entire assembly…The work ahead of (Solomon) is enormous, for the Temple he will build is not just another building–it is for the LORD God himself! Using every resource at my command, I have gathered as much as I could for building the Temple of my God. Now there is enough gold, silver, bronze, iron, and wood, as well as great quantities of onyx, other precious stones, costly jewels, and all kinds of fine stone and marble. And now because of my devotion to the Temple of my God, I am giving all of my own private treasures of gold and silver to help in the construction. This is in addition to the building materials I have already collected for his holy Temple. I am donating…gold…and silver…Now then, who will follow my example? Who is willing to give offerings to the LORD today?" Then the (leaders)…all gave willingly…they gave…gold…gold coins…silver…bronze…iron…and precious stones…The people rejoiced over the offerings, for they had given freely and wholeheartedly to the LORD, and King David was filled with joy. NLT

Where God guides, He provides.
What God orders, He pays for.
God's work, done in God's way,
never lacks God's supply.

In successful God-honoring building projects,
it takes a few extravagantly generous gifts,
combined with dedicated leadership gifts
to make the project one of great rejoicing.

10 Biblical Reasons to Give 10% OR MORE of Your Income to the Lord's Work

As materialism and consumerism have continually infiltrated our lives in recent decades, many people have drifted from any biblical moorings concerning their Christian giving. Here are 10 biblically-based reasons to make giving 10% or more of your income your highest financial priority in life.

1. It is a proven pattern of giving done by Christ followers for many generations. In 1899, a bibliography was compiled of books related to systematic Christian giving. There were over 500 books listed in this bibliography from over 100 years ago, and yet many Christians today do not understand the importance of faithful giving. Scriptures: Genesis 14:17-20, 28:16-22, Leviticus 27:30, Proverbs 3:9-10, Malachi 3:7-15, Matthew 23:23

2. It will help you reverence God more in your life. If you showed me your check book records, I would be able to quickly tell you who or what you feel is important. By giving the best of what you have been given to God, you are expressing your allegiance to Him and you will grow in your respect for the Lord and His working in your life. Scriptures: Deuteronomy 14:23, Malachi 1:6-8

3. It will bring God's wisdom and order to your finances. If I get dressed in the morning and get the first button out of place on my shirt, all the rest of the buttons will be messed up. When it comes to finances, the first button to get in place is your giving. When you get this area in order, everything else follows. Giving is also the only known antidote for "affluenza" (the desire for more things) that permeates our world today. Scriptures: Matthew 6:19-21, 24-34; Luke 12:16-21, I Timothy 6:6-10, 17-19; Ecclesiastes 5:10

4. It will serve as a practical reminder that God is the Owner of everything in your life. By faithfully giving the Lord 10% or more of all you ever receive, you are actively acknowledging His ownership in your life. As someone once told me, "God owns it all and God loans it all." We are not owners, only temporary possessors and managers of what God entrusts to us during our lifetime. Scriptures: I Chronicles 29:11-18, Psalm 24:1-2, 50:10-12, Haggai 2:8

5. It will allow you to experience God's creative provisions. One of the most amazing things about learning to faithfully give to the Lord is the joy so many people have experienced in receiving unexpected blessings in their lives. When you acknowledge God's ownership through your generous giving, you begin to experience His creative provisions in amazing ways. Scriptures: I Kings 17, Proverbs 3:9-10, Malachi 3:7-15, Haggai 1:4-11, 2:15-19; Luke 6:38, Deuteronomy 28, Philippians 4:15-19, Mark 12:41-44

6. It will encourage your spiritual growth and trust in God. There will be times when you will decide to be a faithful giver of what is in your hand, even when you have no idea how you will make it through the coming day, week, or month. But by going ahead and giving to God, your trust in the Lord will grow and you will grow in your ability to see Him provide. Scriptures: Deuteronomy 14:23, Proverbs 3:5-6, Malachi 3:8-10, Haggai 1:4-11, 2:15-19; 2 Corinthians 8:5

7. It will ensure you of treasure in heaven. Jesus encourages you to store up treasure in heaven. The only way to do this is to live generously now. Someone once said, "We can't take it with us, but we can send it on ahead." Scriptures: I Timothy 6:18-19, Matthew 6:19-21, Hebrews 6:10, III John 8, I Samuel 30:22

8. It will strengthen the work of your local church. Many churches struggle for lack of finances. However, when people in a congregation gain a vision for being faithful givers to God at their local church, the whole spirit of a church begins to change – needs are met, people are cared for, more outreach begins to take place, and long-awaited improvements start to happen. God-given momentum builds as people honor the Lord through their giving at church. Scriptures: Acts 2:42-47, 4:32; 2 Corinthians 9:12, 13

9. It will help provide the means to keep your pastor(s) and missionaries in full-time Christian service. It has always been God's plan that his servants are taken care of by his people. Across America and the world, many pastors and missionaries are struggling financially or are even leaving the ministry because of a lack of adequate finances. Your faithful giving can make sure this doesn't happen among the pastors or missionaries you know. Scriptures: I Corinthians 9:9-11,14; I Timothy 5:17-18, III John 5-8, Philemon 4:15-19, Galatians 6:6, Luke 8:3, II Kings 4:8-10

10. It will help accomplish needed building projects and renovations. Some of the most exciting times in the life of a church or ministry occur when facilities are being improved or expanded. But for building projects to succeed, large extraordinary gifts are needed. Building projects only happen well with special gifts that are "above and beyond" people's normal giving. Scriptures: 2 Chronicles 24:4-14, Exodus 35,36; II Kings 12:2-16, Ezra 1:4-6, I Chronicles 29:2-19

DAY 17
Life does not consist in the abundance of your possessions.

Think about, discuss or pray about the verse that relates most to your life:

Luke 12:15 Jesus said to them, "Watch out! Be on your guard against all kinds of greed; a man's life does not consist in the abundance of his possessions."

Joshua 7:21-26 Achan said, "When I saw…a beautiful robe… silver…gold, I coveted them and took them. They are hidden in the ground inside my tent…Then all Israel stoned Achan…"

1 Timothy 6:6-8 Do you want to be truly rich? You already are if you are happy and good. After all, we didn't bring any money with us when we came into the world, and we can't carry away a single penny when we die. So we should be well satisfied without money if we have enough food and clothing.

Psalm 62:10 Though your riches increase, don't set your heart on them.

Psalm 119:36-37 Turn my heart toward your statutes and not toward selfish gain. Turn my eyes away from worthless things.

Psalm 37:16 Better the little that the righteous have than the wealth of many wicked.

Proverbs 15:16 Better a little with the fear of the LORD than great wealth with turmoil.

If you want to feel rich,
just count all the things you have that money can't buy.

The most important things in life aren't things
and the best things in life are always free.

DAY 18
Give in proportion to how God has blessed you materially.

Think about, discuss or pray about the verse that relates most to your life:

Ezra 2:69 According to their ability they gave to the treasury for this work.

Deuteronomy 16:10 Bring God a free-will offering proportionate in size to his blessing upon you as judged by the amount of your harvest.

Mark 12:44 They all gave out of their wealth.

Act 11:29 The disciples, each according to his ability, decided to provide help.

2 Corinthians 8:12 For if the willingness is there, the gift is acceptable according to what one has, not according to what he does not have.

2 Corinthians 8:3 They gave as much as they were able, and even beyond their ability.

1 Corinthians 16:2 Let each one of you give according to how the Lord has prospered you.

Matthew 2:11 (The wise men) bowed down and worshipped him. Then they opened their treasures and presented him with gifts of gold, incense and myrrh.

You should give according to your income,
lest God make your income
according to your giving.

DAY 19
Women play a significant part in giving to God's work.

Think about, discuss or pray about the verse that relates most to your life:

Luke 8:3 Joanna the wife of Cuza, the manager of Herod's household; Susanna; and many others. These women were helping to support them (Jesus and his disciples) out of their own means.

Mark 14:3 A woman came with an alabaster jar of very expensive perfume (worth a year's wages), made of pure nard. She broke the jar and poured the perfume on (Jesus') head.

Exodus 35:21,22,25,26 Everyone who was willing and whose heart moved him came and brought an offering to the LORD for the work… All who were willing, men and women alike, came and brought gold jewelry of all kinds: brooches, earrings, rings and ornaments. They all presented their gold as a wave offering to the LORD… Every skilled woman spun with her hands and brought what she had spun– blue, purple or scarlet yarn or fine linen. And all the women who were willing and had the skill spun the goat hair.

Acts 9:36-39 In Joppa there was a disciple named Tabitha, who was always doing good and helping the poor.

Nehemiah 2:6-8 Then the king, with the queen sitting beside him, asked me (Nehemiah), "How long will your journey take, and when will you get back?" It pleased the king to send me; so I set a time…and because the gracious hand of my God was upon me, the king granted my requests.

1 Timothy 5:9-10 No widow may be put on the list of widows unless she is over sixty, has been faithful to her husband, and is well known for her good deeds, such as bringing up children, showing hospitality, washing the feet of the saints, helping those in trouble and devoting herself to all kinds of good deeds.

*God looks at the heart,
not the hand–the giver, not the gift.*

DAY 20
Beware of greed, hoarding or selfishness in your life.

Think about, discuss or pray about the verse that relates most to your life:

Luke 12:15-21 (Jesus said) "Beware! Don't be greedy for what you don't have. Real life is not measured by how much we own." And he gave an illustration: "A rich man had a fertile farm that produced fine crops. In fact, his barns were full to overflowing. So he said, `I know! I'll tear down my barns and build bigger ones. Then I'll have room enough to store everything. And I'll sit back and say to myself, My friend, you have enough stored away for years to come. Now take it easy! Eat, drink, and be merry!' "But God said to him, `You fool! You will die this very night. Then who will get it all?' "Yes, a person is a fool to store up earthly wealth but not have a rich relationship with God." NLT

James 5:1-3 Now listen, you rich people, weep and wail because of the misery that is coming upon you. Your wealth has rotted, and moths have eaten your clothes. Your gold and silver are corroded. Their corrosion will testify against you and eat your flesh like fire. You have hoarded wealth in the last days.

2 Corinthians 9:6-7 Whoever sows sparingly will also reap sparingly, and whoever sows generously will also reap generously. Each man should give what he has decided in his heart to give, not reluctantly or under compulsion, for God loves a cheerful giver.

There are no pockets in a shroud and no U-hauls behind a hearse.

God is going to have to take some people to heaven feet first, because they keep trying to hold onto everything they have here on earth.

DAY 21
Give careful thought to your financial practices and never neglect God's house and servants.

Think about, discuss or pray about the verse that relates most to your life:

Haggai 1:4-12 "Is it a time for you yourselves to be living in your paneled houses, while this house remains a ruin?" Now this is what the LORD Almighty says: "Give careful thought to your ways. You have planted much, but have harvested little. You eat, but never have enough. You drink, but never have your fill. You put on clothes, but are not warm. You earn wages, only to put them in a purse with holes in it." This is what the LORD Almighty says: "Give careful thought to your ways. Go up into the mountains and bring down timber and build the house, so that I may take pleasure in it and be honored," says the LORD. "You expected much, but see, it turned out to be little. What you brought home, I blew away. Why?" declares the LORD Almighty. "Because of my house, which remains a ruin, while each of you is busy with his own house. Therefore, because of you the heavens have withheld their dew and the earth its crops. I called for a drought on the fields and the mountains, on the grain, the new wine, the oil and whatever the ground produces, on men and cattle, and on the labor of your hands."

Nehemiah 10:39 (The leaders and the people repented and said) "We will not neglect the house of our God."

Exodus 22:29 (God says) "You must be prompt in giving Me the tithe."

Deuteronomy 12:19 Be careful not to neglect the Levites (ministers) as long as you live in your land.

Materialism is to generosity what kryptonite was to Superman.

If everyone in your church followed your pattern of giving, would your church receive a token, a tip or a tithe?

THE AMAZING STORY OF A MILLIONAIRE GIVER

A few years ago, I heard a man named Steve from California speak at a Christian conference. He told the story about how he and his wife became millionaire givers!

Steve owned a small business and made about $50,000 a year. He went to a Campus Crusade for Christ conference and heard Dr. Bill Bright challenge everyone in the audience to each give a $1,000,000 to the Lord's work. After the message, he went up to Dr. Bright and asked, "Obviously, you didn't really mean that my wife and I should be included in the people that will give a million dollars to the Lord's work?" Dr. Bright asked, "How much did you make last year?" Steve said, "$50,000." Dr. Bright asked him how much he gave to the Lord last year. Steve said "$15,000." Steve thought Dr. Bright would be impressed that he gave more than 25% of his income to the Lord's work. Dr. Bright said, "Well, next year, trust God to allow you to give $50,000." But Steve said, "That's my entire salary!" Dr. Bright said, "Trust God and if he provides you with the funds, give $50,000!"

Steve went home and amazingly his little business did well and he and his young family lived on their $50,000 salary and they gave $50,000 to the Lord's work! The next year, by faith they pledged to themselves and the Lord that they would continue to live on $50,000 but would seek to give $100,000 to the Lord's work if God provided it. Amazingly, through some unbelievable circumstances and a great testing of their faith, they were able to give $100,000 that year.

Each year, they continued to live on their basic salary and give their extra income to the Lord's work. And believe it or not, within five years, they had given over a million dollars to the Lord!

Sometimes God gives us more income not to increase our standard of living, but to increase our standard of giving.

"From what you have, take an offering for the LORD."
Exodus 35:5

Step 1 Check ☑ all items that you have on the asset list.

Step 2 Estimate the financial value of the items you checked.

Step 3 Circle any possible items and resources you no longer need OR that could be given/sold/used for the Lord's work.

Step 4 Determine the "Offering" value of any of the items you circled (if they were partially or totally given to the Lord's work).

Step 5 Begin to think about how to give identified items:
- Should I give or transfer the physical item to the Lord's work (and the ministry can choose to use it or sell it)?
- Should I seek to sell the item (personally sell, classified ads, ebay, etc.) and give some or all of the proceeds to the Lord's work?

IMPORTANT NOTE: In transferring assets, it is wise to talk with the ministry(s) you want to help to determine how to best give an asset to the Lord's work.

Depending on the size and type of asset, it may be wise to have the ministry assist you in obtaining the help of experienced estate planning professional to determine how to most effectively and affordably "transfer" an asset to be utilized by a ministry.

☑	LIST OF GOD-GIVEN ASSETS	VALUE	OFFERING?
☐	Vehicle(s)		
☐	Checking account(s) & cash		
☐	CDs or savings accounts		
☐	Motorcycles/recreational vehicles		
☐	Motor home/RV/trailer/camper		
☐	Boats/watercraft & accessories		
☐	Home value		
☐	Timeshare/condo/vacation home		
☐	Sports, exercise, or hunting equipment		
☐	Workshop or garage tools & equipment		
☐	Craft or camera equipment & supplies		
☐	Musical instruments		
☐	Appliances/furniture/furnishings		
☐	Jewelry or gems or furs		
☐	Antiques, memorabilia or heirlooms		
☐	Artwork		
☐	Books/videos/albums		
☐	China/crystal/glassware/silver/etc.		
☐	Stocks		
☐	Bonds		
☐	Mutual funds		
☐	US Notes/bills/bonds		
☐	Commodities		
☐	Pension funds		
☐	Military pension funds		
☐	IRA or Keogh retirement accounts		
☐	401(k) or 403(b) retirement accounts		
☐	College savings funds		
☐	Collections (coins/stamps/crafts/toys)		
☐	Trust fund(s) or inheritance funds		
☐	Livestock, animals		
☐	Rental properties		
☐	Business, farm, ranch: Buildings/land		
☐	Business: Vehicles/equipment/supplies		
☐	Undeveloped land or farmland		
☐	Items in storage units		
☐	RV pad or boat dock		
☐	Foundation or donor advised funds		
☐	Business partnerships/ownership		
☐	Real estate partnerships		
☐	Other:		

Week 3
SHARING YOUR TREASURES

Possible questions to think about or discuss

1. Growing up, what was a possession that you really, really wanted and then finally got? Did it bring as much satisfaction and significance to your life as you were expecting? Where is the item today?

2. Are you more of a pack-rat or a throw-it-out type of person? Why? Are the Scriptures you've been reading causing you to reconsider or reinforce your attitude and practices? Why?

3. When you filled out the "Assets" worksheet for this week's project, what surprised you or caught your attention in doing this exercise?

4. If you think back to one of the most financially generous things you ever did for the Lord's work, what was it?

5. Have you ever regretted any giving you've done to the Lord's work?

6. What truth or Bible verse from the past seven days of reading stood out to you the most?

7. What are your three largest financial assets?

8. What did you think of the millionaire giver's story? If you could give a million dollars to the Lord's work over 5 years, where would you give it?

9. Have you ever sold something in order to be more generous to a special need for the Lord's work?

10. Have you ever given away a possession to help in the Lord's work or to help a person in need? What did you give away? How did it make you feel?

Week 4

*The whole Bible was given to us by
inspiration from God and is useful
to teach us what is true and to
make us realize what is wrong
in our lives; it straightens us
out and helps us do what
is right.*[TLB]

2 Timothy 3:16

DAY 22
God has a high regard for a Christian in humble financial circumstances.

Think about, discuss or pray about the verse that relates most to your life:

James 1:9-11 The brother in humble circumstances ought to take pride in his high position. But the one who is rich should take pride in his low position, because he will pass away like a wild flower. For the sun rises with scorching heat and withers the plant; its blossom falls and its beauty is destroyed. In the same way, the rich man will fade away even while he goes about his business.

James 2:5-6 Listen, my dear brothers: Has not God chosen those who are poor in the eyes of the world to be rich in faith and to inherit the kingdom he promised those who love him? But you have insulted the poor. Is it not the rich who are exploiting you?

2 Corinthians 8:2-4 Though (the Macedonian Christians) have been going through much trouble and hard times, they have mixed their wonderful joy with their deep poverty, and the result has been an overflow of giving to others. They gave not only what they could afford but far more; and I can testify that they did it because they wanted to…They begged us to take the money so they could share in the joy of helping the Christians in Jerusalem.

I am only one,
But still I am one.
I cannot do everything,
But still I can do something.
And because I cannot do everything,
I will not refuse to do the something that I can do.

Edward Hale 1822

DAY 23
God has good works for you to do during your lifetime.

Think about, discuss or pray about the verse that relates most to your life:

Ephesians 2:10 For we are God's workmanship, created in Christ Jesus to do good works, which God prepared in advance for us to do.

Esther 4:14 (Mordecai said to Esther) "If you remain silent at this time, relief and deliverance for the Jews will arise from another place, but you and your father's family will perish. And who knows but that you have come to royal position for such a time as this?"

Matthew 5:16 In the same way, let your light shine before men, that they may see your good deeds and praise your Father in heaven.

2 Corinthians 9:8, 11 God is able to make all grace abound to you, so that in all things at all times, having all that you need, you will abound in every good work…You will be made rich in every way so that you can be generous on every occasion, and through us your generosity will result in thanksgiving to God. .

1 Timothy 6:18-19 Tell the rich to use their money to do good. They should be rich in good works and should give happily to those in need, always being ready to share with others whatever God has given them. By doing this they will be storing up real treasure for themselves in heaven– it is the only safe investment for eternity! And they will be living a fruitful Christian life down here as well.

Hebrews 10:24 In response to all he has done for us, let us outdo each other in being helpful and kind to each other and in doing good.

*Many people go to their graves,
with God's unplayed music still inside of them.
Don't waste your God-given life
with low living, small planning, mundane talking,
constant grumbling or cheap giving.
Be all that God has called you and equipped you to be.*

God's Creative Provisions

Experiencing God as Your Provider

The earth is the LORD's, and everything in it. *Psalm 24:1*

One of the most amazing discoveries you will make as you begin to more faithfully and generously give to God's work at your church and beyond, is that God will begin to show himself as your provider in unique and creative ways.

While I am not an advocate of the prosperity gospel and the health and wealth religion promoted by some TV evangelists, I have seen that people who honor God in their giving experience God's blessings in a variety of ways. Since the Bible clearly teaches that God owns EVERYTHING, He can be very creative in how He goes about providing for your needs.

Scriptures that have shaped my understanding and experience of God's creative provisions include:

- *Proverbs 13:22* A sinner's wealth is stored up for the righteous.

- *Ecclesiastes 2:26* To the sinner, God gives the task of gathering and storing up wealth to hand it over to the one who pleases God.

- *Job 27:16-17* Evil people may have all the money in the world, and they may store away mounds of clothing. But the righteous will wear that clothing.

- *Isaiah 45:3* I will give you the treasures of darkness, riches stored in secret places.

In these verses and in my experience of walking with the Lord, I have seen that He often "transfers the ownership" of specifically needed items without cost or at significant savings to faithful givers.

Many people think that their meets are met through their paycheck, and not necessarily from God. While God may use a person's wages to provide for many needs, God is so much bigger than a paycheck! A company may be your employer, but God is your true provider.

I encourage you to pray and ask God to lead you to His provisions to meet your needs. The Lord may choose to use your current income, savings, increased income, or He may lead you to the very item you need without cost or at a significant savings.

Some ways I have seen the Lord creatively provide beyond a regular paycheck includes:

Needed items provided through friends, relatives, neighbors, or other Christians: As people move through the different seasons of life, they often have possessions they no longer need. They are often willing to give away or sell items at significant savings to someone they know could use them.

Inheritances, bonuses, and scholarships: I have known of people that have been totally surprised by amounts of money they have unexpectedly received from relatives, employers, or educational institutions.

Retail stores and manufacturers: In today's tight retail economy, there are many sales that will allow you to experience 40-90% off through sales, clearance racks, overruns, returns, floor models, and demo merchandise.

Bankruptcies, estate sales, repossessions, and auctions: While you have to know the market value ahead of time, these outlets for merchandise, vehicles, housing, etc. can be great sources for God-given provisions.

Government: There are many ways a government program can be used by God to directly benefit someone.

Consignment shops, thrift shops, and garage sales: Often you can get quality or functional merchandise for 50-95% off the retail price through these sources.

As you become more of a faithful and generous giver, be sure to pray about God's provision for your own needs, and don't be surprised at the creative ways He may supply for you!

DAY 24
Some people are called to extravagant giving.

Think about, discuss or pray about the verse that relates most to your life:

Mark 10:21-25 Jesus looked at him (the young rich man) and loved him. "One thing you lack," he said. "Go, sell everything you have and give to the poor, and you will have treasure in heaven. Then come, follow me." At this the man's face fell. He went away sad, because he had great wealth. Jesus looked around and said to his disciples, "How hard it is for the rich to enter the kingdom of God!" The disciples were amazed at his words. But Jesus said again, "Children, how hard it is to enter the kingdom of God! It is easier for a camel to go through the eye of a needle than for a rich man to enter the kingdom of God."

1 Kings 19:19-21 So Elijah went from there and found Elisha. He was plowing with twelve yoke of oxen, and he himself was driving the twelfth pair. Elijah went up to him and threw his cloak around him. Elisha then left his oxen and ran after Elijah. He took his yoke of oxen and slaughtered them. He burned the plowing equipment to cook the meat and gave it to the people, and they ate. Then he set out to follow Elijah and became his attendant.

Mark 14:3 A woman came with an alabaster jar of very expensive perfume (worth a year's wages), made of pure nard. She broke the jar and poured the perfume on (Jesus') head.

Acts 4:34-37 From time to time those who owned lands or houses sold them, brought the money from the sales and put it at the apostles' feet, and it was distributed to anyone as he had need. Joseph, a Levite from Cyprus, whom the apostles called Barnabas (which means Son of Encouragement), sold a field he owned and brought the money and put it at the apostles' feet.

What is the most precious and financially valuable item(s) in your life? Would you ever consider giving this item so you could worship the Lord through extravagant generosity?

DAY 25
God can do great things through one person or a group that is devoted to Him.

Think about, discuss or pray about the verse that relates most to your life:

2 Chronicles 16:9 The eyes of the Lord search back and forth across the whole earth, looking for people whose hearts are perfect toward him, so that he can show his great power in helping them.

1 Samuel 14:6-13 "Let's go across to see those pagans," Jonathan said to his armor bearer. " The LORD will help us, for nothing can hinder the LORD. He can win a battle whether he has many warriors or only a few!" …So they climbed up using both hands and feet, and the Philistines fell back as Jonathan and his armor bearer killed them right and left.

Judges 7:7 The LORD said to Gideon, "With the three hundred men that lapped I will save you and give the (120,000) Midianites into your hands."

2 Chronicles 14:9,11 Zerah marched out against (God's people) with a vast army…Then Asa called to the LORD his God and said, "LORD, there is no one like you to help the powerless against the mighty. Help us, O LORD our God, for we rely on you, and in your name we have come against this vast army. O LORD, you are our God; do not let man prevail against you."… (and) The LORD struck down the Cushites.

Zech 4:6 "Not by might nor by power, but by my Spirit," says the LORD Almighty.

1 Samuel 17:45-47 David shouted (to Goliath), "You come to me with sword, spear, and javelin, but I come to you in the name of the LORD Almighty, whom you have defied. Today the LORD will conquer you, and I will kill you and cut off your head….And everyone will know that the LORD does not need weapons to rescue his people. It is his battle, not ours. The LORD will give you to us!"

Expect great things from God. Attempt great things for God.

DAY 26
God blesses you financially so that you can be a blessing to others.

Think about, discuss or pray about the verse that relates most to your life:

Proverbs 10:16 The good man's earnings advance the cause of righteousness. The evil man squanders his on sin.

Psalm 67:7 God will bless us. And peoples from remotest lands will worship him.

Proverbs 11:24 It is possible to give away and become richer! It is also possible to hold on too tightly and lose everything. Yes, the liberal man shall be rich! By watering others, he waters himself.

Deuteronomy 15:7-8, 10-11 If there is a poor man among your brothers in any of the towns of the land that the LORD your God is giving you, do not be hardhearted or tightfisted toward your poor brother….Rather be openhanded and freely lend him whatever he needs. Give generously to him and do so without a grudging heart; then because of this the LORD your God will bless you in all your work and in everything you put your hand to.

Hebrews 6:10-11 God is not unjust; he will not forget your work and the love you have shown him as you have helped his people and continue to help them.

2 Corinthians 9:8 God is able to make all grace abound to you, so that in all things at all times, having all that you need, you will abound in every good work.

*Do your givin'
while you are livin'
then you're knowin'
where it's goin'.*

DAY 27
It is appropriate to ask people how you can help them.

Think about, discuss or pray about the verse that relates most to your life:

Nehemiah 2:2-8 The king asked me, "Why are you so sad? You aren't sick, are you? You look like a man with deep troubles." Then I was badly frightened, but I replied, "Long live the king! Why shouldn't I be sad? For the city where my ancestors are buried is in ruins, and the gates have been burned down." The king asked, "Well, how can I help you?" With a prayer to the God of heaven, I replied, "If it please Your Majesty and if you are pleased with me, your servant, send me to Judah to rebuild the city where my ancestors are buried…And the king granted these requests, because the gracious hand of God was on me. NLT

Matthew 20:30-34 Two blind men were sitting by the roadside, and when they heard that Jesus was going by, they shouted, "Lord, Son of David, have mercy on us!…Jesus stopped and called them. "What do you want me to do for you?" He asked. "Lord," they answered, "we want our sight." Jesus had compassion on them and touched their eyes. Immediately they received their sight and followed him.

Mark 10:51-52 "What do you want me to do for you?" Jesus asked him. The blind man said, "Rabbi, I want to see." "Go," said Jesus, "your faith has healed you." Immediately he received his sight and followed Jesus along the road.

Do all the good you can, by all the means you can,
in all the ways you can, in all the places you can,
at all the times you can, to all the people you can,
as long as you can.

John Wesley

DAY 28
God will reward you for your faithful generosity and diligent labors.

Think about, discuss or pray about the verse that relates most to your life:

1 Corinthians 15:58 Therefore, my dear brothers, stand firm. Let nothing move you. Always give yourselves fully to the work of the Lord, because you know that your labor in the Lord is not in vain.

Galatians 6:9-10 Let us not get tired of doing what is right, for after a while we will reap a harvest of blessing if we don't get discouraged and give up. That's why whenever we can we should always be kind to everyone, and especially to our Christian brothers.

Hebrews 6:10-12 God is not unjust; he will not forget your work and the love you have shown him as you have helped his people and continue to help them. We want each of you to show this same diligence to the very end, in order to make your hope sure. We do not want you to become lazy, but to imitate those who through faith and patience inherit what has been promised.

Philippians 4:17 Not that I am looking for a gift, but I am looking for what may be credited to your account.

Giving is a giant lever positioned on the fulcrum of this world, allowing us to move mountains in the next world. Because we give, eternity will be different—for others and for us.
Randy Alcorn

I have watched over 100,000 families over my years of investment counseling. I always saw greater prosperity and happiness among those families who tithed than among those who didn't.
Sir John Templeton

Just Like In Monopoly, It All Goes Back In the Box

"Naked I came from my mother's womb, and naked I will depart" Job 1:21

When Charles B. Darrow proposed a new board game called Monopoly to Parker Brothers in 1934, the all-knowing executives rejected it due to "52 design errors"! But Darrow, a true believer, started printing and selling the game himself. The rest is history.

John Ortberg writes of growing up with a grandmother who was a ruthless competitor at Monopoly. She played against her grandchildren and won nearly every time.

But one day young John managed to win. As most kids will do, he made the most of his rare victory; he raked all the play money, tokens and markers toward him and gloated arrogantly in his triumph.

The grandmother smiled and said, "Just remember, John— it all goes back in the box. All the money, all the hotels and motels and game tokens; at the end of the game, it all goes back in the box!" SOURCE: MEN OF INTEGRITY MAGAZINE,

Realize that everything you have, must go back in the box!
You have to leave everything to someone.
Isn't it wise to give during your lifetime to the
Someone who gave you everything you have?
And remember: A shroud has no pockets. And although
you can't take it with you, you can send it on ahead!

IDENTIFY: "WHAT MINISTRIES AND PROJECTS DO YOU CARE ABOUT AND WANT TO SUPPORT?"

*"You are generous because of your faith.
And I am praying that you will really put your generosity to
work, for in so doing you will come to an understanding
of all the good things we can do for Christ."* NLT
Philemon 1:6

*"You will be made rich in every way so that you
can be generous on every occasion."*
2 Corinthians 9:11

Step 1 List the church and Christian ministries, missionaries, and organizations you are currently supporting.

Step 2 After prayer, circle any existing ministry you support OR a new ministry opportunity that could best utilize your increased or sacrificial support.

Step 3 Determine "future" priorities or amounts based on how you believe God is leading you.

SUGGESTION: If you tithe to the Lord's work, consider tithing your normal expected income (your main income source) to your local church. Then consider giving 10% or more from all your other income sources to support other ministries and special needs or projects that God lays on your heart.

MINISTRIES YOU SUPPORT	PAST $ SUPPORT	FUTURE SUPPORT
Your local church		
Benevolence offerings/helping the needy		
Building project		

Church Ministries: Pastoral staff, missions, benevolence, youth, children, adult, women, men, facilities, media, denomination, etc.

Ministry Buildings & Equipment: New facilities, relocation, expansion, renovations, vehicles, computers, program equipment, etc.

Needy: Widows, homeless, urban ministries, crisis pregnancy, prisoners, refugees, relief, orphans, rescue missions, disabilities, scholarships, etc.

Education: Christian schools, Bible schools, colleges, seminaries, etc

Missions: Foreign missionaries, state-side missionaries, international mission organizations, church planting, theological education, relief, leadership training and development, economic development, facilities, denomination missionaries, etc.

Outreach/Discipleship: Evangelism, evangelistic crusades, media, magazines, books, TV, radio, financial, campus, professional groups, sports, men, women, children, teens, camps, conference centers, etc.

Week 4
SHARING YOUR TREASURES

Possible questions to think about or discuss

1. Are you a systematic giver, a spontaneous giver or a little of both?

2. If you have children, what have you done to help them become faithful and generous givers?

3. Have you experienced any of God's creative provisions mentioned on page 52?

4. When you filled out the "Giving" worksheet for this week's project, what surprised you or caught your attention in doing this exercise?

5. How have you determined how much you will give to your local church? How do you give (cash, weekly, bi-weekly, monthly, yearly, sporadically, loose cash you have on you, etc.)?

6. What other types of ministries or needs do you like to give to?

7. Do you take into consideration the tax implications of your giving? Why or why not?

8. What truth or Bible verse from the past seven days of reading stood out to you the most?

9. How do you make sure you are faithful in your giving to the Lord (i.e. write the check/s monthly, keep track in a bookkeeping program, put the Lord's money in a special place, electronic giving, etc.)?

10. If married, do you agree together on whatever giving you are going to do OR does each person have freedom to give OR is there one of you that is the main decider of where and how much you'll give?

11. If you have children, do your children know how much you give, where you give and why you give? Why or why not?

Week 5

The word of God is living and active. Sharper than any double-edged sword... it judges the thoughts and attitudes of the heart.

Hebrews 4:12

DAY 29

The giver and the front-line worker are equal partners in God's work.

Think about, discuss or pray about the verse that relates most to your life:

1 Samuel 30:24 The share of the man who stayed with the supplies is to be the same as that of him who went down to the battle. All will share alike.

3 John 1:5-8 You are faithful in what you are doing for the brothers, even though they are strangers to you. They have told the church about your love. You will do well to send them on their way in a manner worthy of God…We ought therefore to show hospitality to such men so that we may work together for the truth.

1 Corinthians 3:7-9 Neither he who plants nor he who waters is anything, but only God, who makes things grow. The man who plants and the man who waters have one purpose, and each will be rewarded according to his own labor. For we are God's fellow workers.

Philippians 4:17 Not that I am looking for a gift, but I am looking for what may be credited to your account.

Matthew 10:41-42 (Jesus said) "Anyone who receives a prophet because he is a prophet will receive a prophet's reward, and anyone who receives a righteous man because he is a righteous man will receive a righteous man's reward."

I judge all things only by the price
they shall gain in eternity.
John Wesley

Only one life, 'twill soon be past;
only what's done for Christ will last.
Missionary C. T Studd

DAY 30
Your giving will be a great help and encouragement to others.

Think about, discuss or pray about the verse that relates most to your life:

2 Corinthians 9:12-14 This service that you perform is not only supplying the needs of God's people but is also overflowing in many expressions of thanks to God. Because of the service by which you have proved yourselves, men will praise God for the obedience that accompanies your confession of the gospel of Christ, and for your generosity in sharing with them and with everyone else.

Acts 4:34-37 There were no needy persons among them. For from time to time those who owned lands or houses sold them, brought the money from the sales and put it at the apostles' feet, and it was distributed to anyone as he had need. Joseph…whom the apostles called Barnabas (which means Son of Encouragement), sold a field he owned and brought the money and put it at the apostles' feet.

Proverbs 19:4,6 Wealth brings many friends. Everyone is the friend of a man who gives gifts.

Matthew 5:14-16 You are the light of the world…let your light shine before men, that they may see your good deeds and praise your Father in heaven.

There is no advantage in being the richest person in the cemetery.

A wealthy Christian man who lost everything in a financial downturn was asked if he ever regretted all the giving he had done to the Lord's work. He replied, "What I gave, I still have. What I kept, I lost."

Excel in the Grace of Giving

Crossing lines in the sand to give more generously

Wherever you are in your journey to a more generous life,
God wants to take you further!

The Bible says in 2 Corinthians 8:7, "Just as you excel in everything…see that you also excel in this grace of giving." I have discovered that the Lord will draw a new line in the sand for each of us to cross over in order to live more generously and to experience Him more fully. Every step of the way, God calls us to consider the resources He has placed in our hands. Then, He invites us to release them for His work and to trust Him to be our provider. At each point, we may find ourselves fearful and want to hold on to what we have instead of letting it go and trusting God with our needs. In my life, these lines in the sand to become more generous have included the following:

Giving more than I thought I could afford to give. As a young man who had recently come to a personal faith in Jesus Christ, I was prompted in my heart during a church service to put a $20 bill in the offering plate. Prior to that time, I had never given more than a few dollars. As I wrestled with this prompting, I contemplated putting the $20 bill in and taking out change! Ultimately, with a shaking hand, I gave the $20 (without taking change) and in the next few days I experienced God's peace and provision in such a way that I did not regret giving that amount.

Giving even while I was in debt. There was a season in my life when my bills had piled up so high that I had more month than I had money! It was during this time that I was prompted in my heart to start giving 10% of my income to the Lord. This didn't make sense to me since I didn't have enough money to pay my bills and take care of my needs every month. But I decided to trust God and cross over this new line in the sand to live and give more generously. The next time I received a paycheck, the first check I wrote (hesitantly) was a check for 10% to the Lord's work. As I continued to do this, I noticed that I was not as foolish with my money, I had a greater trust in God to provide for my needs, and I began to make progress in paying off my debts. I also joined a Crown Financial Ministries Bible study (www.crown.org) and learned how to prayerfully develop a spending plan to help me get out of debt completely within a few years.

65

Giving a large gift that was worth half a year's salary. As a young couple, my wife and I were prompted to sacrificially give a gift from our savings account to help a Christian ministry. At the time, this five-figure gift was worth more than a half a year's salary. As we prayed and discussed this giving opportunity, we decided to write a list of all the things we would be giving up if we gave this gift. We prayed and decided that this was a new line in the sand that God was calling us to cross. Again, with a bit of a shaking hand, I wrote the check. A few years later, we found the list we had written and we were amazed to discover that God had graciously and unexpectedly provided for every item on the list that we thought we had given up. Through this experience we learned that you can never out give God. Another time, the Lord led us to give another gift that was equal to a year's salary.

Giving increased offerings by "Counting Our Blessings." For years, we would sit down on Sunday nights with a pencil and notebook and list the ways God had provided for us over the last seven days (e.g., my main income, my wife's substitute teaching income, unexpected financial income/ gifts, discounts on purchases, hospitality/help we experienced, and more). Based on what we recorded, we would give 10% of my expected salary to our church and give 10% or more of the other financial blessings to other Christian causes and needs.

Giving more by limiting our lifestyle. There was a season in our lives when we were making more than we ever dreamed possible. During this time, we felt God's new line in the sand for us was to limit our lifestyle spending so we could increase our giving. We decided that we would limit our lifestyle spending to a specific annual amount and that ALL monies received over this amount would be given 100% to the Lord's work. To do this, we opened up two different checking accounts. The first check book was for our living expenses (a set amount each month) and the other check book was for our increased giving. God ultimately used this decision and allowed us to not only increase our giving, but also for me to accept a Senior Pastor position at a salary that was 65% less than we were making.

Giving more by giving higher percentages of our income. From this booklet, you see that I believe that giving 10% to the Lord's work is the starting blocks and not the finish line of faithful biblical giving. In my own life and in the lives of generous people I've known, I've learned that by giving 10%, it is much easier to obey God's promptings and learn to give higher percentages of income and assets to the Lord's work in the future.

What about you? What "line in the sand" is God calling you to cross at this time in order for you to live a more generous life and excel in the grace of giving?

DAY 31
Your pursuit of God and a generous life will give you a fuller and richer life.

Think about, discuss or pray about the verse that relates most to your life:

1 Timothy 6:18-19 Command them to do good, to be rich in good deeds, and to be generous and willing to share. In this way they will lay up treasure for themselves as a firm foundation for the coming age, so that they may take hold of the life that is truly life.

Philemon 1:6-7 You are generous because of your faith. And I am praying that you will really put your generosity to work, for in so doing you will come to an understanding of all the good things we can do for Christ. I myself have gained much joy and comfort from your love, my brother, because your kindness has so often refreshed the hearts of God's people.

John 10:10 (Jesus said) "I have come that they may have life, and have it to the full."

3 John 2-3 Beloved, I pray that you may prosper in all things and be in health, just as your soul prospers.

Matthew 6:33 (God) will give you all you need from day to day if |you live for him and make the Kingdom of God your primary concern.

First things belong to God.
The first day of the week belongs to God.
The first hour of the day belongs to God.
The first portion of your income belongs to God.
When you make God first, He can help you.

James MacDonald

DAY 32
Realize that God will bring specific people into your life that you can truly help.

Think about, discuss or pray about the verse that relates most to your life:

James 2:15-16 Suppose a brother or sister is without clothes and daily food. If one of you says to him, "Go, I wish you well; keep warm and well fed," but does nothing about his physical needs, what good is it?

Proverbs 14:31 Whoever is kind to the needy honors God.

Luke 14:13-14 When you give a banquet, invite the poor, crippled, lame, and the blind, and you will be blessed. Although they cannot repay you, you will be repaid at the resurrection of the righteous.

Deuteronomy. 15:7-11 If there is a poor man among your brothers in any of the towns of the land that the LORD your God is giving you, do not be hardhearted or tightfisted toward your poor brother. Rather be openhanded and freely lend him whatever he needs...Give generously to him and do so without a grudging heart; then because of this the LORD your God will bless you in all your work and in everything you put your hand to. There will always be poor people in the land. Therefore I command you to be openhanded toward your brothers and toward the poor and needy in your land.

*You've heard of prayer warriors.
What about giving warriors?
God has entrusted us with so much.
Perhaps He is raising up a great army of givers,
and He's calling us to enlist.*

Randy Alcorn

DAY 33
Any wealth gained by the wrong means has serious consequences.

Think about, discuss or pray about the verse that relates most to your life:

Job 20:17-24 (The wicked man) shall not enjoy the goods he stole…His labors shall not be rewarded; wealth will give him no joy. For he has oppressed the poor and foreclosed their homes; he will never recover. Though he was always greedy, now he has nothing; of all the things he dreamed of – none remain. Because he stole at every opportunity, his prosperity shall not continue. He shall run into trouble at the peak of his powers; all the wicked shall destroy him…God will rain down wrath upon him. He will be chased and struck down.

Proverbs 11:1-5 The Lord hates cheating and delights in honesty. Proud men end in shame…the evil man is destroyed by his dishonesty. Riches won't help you on Judgment Day…the wicked shall fall beneath their load of sins.

Job 27:19-20 (The wicked) goes to bed rich but wakes up to find that all his wealth is gone. Terror overwhelms him, and he is blown away in the storms of the night.

Proverbs 13:11 Dishonest money dwindles away.

Jeremiah 17:11 Like a bird that fills her nest with young she has not hatched and which will soon desert her and fly away, so is the man who gets his wealth by unjust means. Sooner or later he will lose his riches and at the end of his life become a poor old fool.

Hosea 12:8 Ephraim boasts, "I am so rich! I have gotten it all by myself!" But riches can't make up for sin.

*How much better to be honestly poor
than questionably rich.*

DAY 34
Realize God can use anyone and any resources to provide for His work.

Think about, discuss or pray about the verse that relates most to your life:

Proverbs 13:22 A sinner's wealth is stored up for the righteous.

Ecclesiastes 2:26 To the man who pleases him, God gives wisdom, knowledge and happiness, but to the sinner he gives the task of gathering and storing up wealth to hand it over to the one who pleases God.

Isaiah 45:3 (God says) "I will give you the treasures of darkness, riches stored in secret places, so that you may know that I am the LORD…who summons you by name."

Job 27:13, 16, 17 Here is the fate God allots to the wicked, the heritage a ruthless man receives from the Almighty: …Though he heaps up silver like dust and clothes like piles of clay, what he lays up the righteous will wear, and the innocent will divide his silver.

Proverbs 28:8 Income from exploiting the poor will end up in the hands of someone who pities them.

Isaiah 23:18 Her profit and her earnings will be set apart for the LORD; they will not be stored up or hoarded. Her profits will go to those who live before the LORD.

The world has yet to see what God can do with a man fully consecrated to Him.

Dwight L. Moody

DAY 35
Your giving in this life will have an impact on your experiences in eternity.

Think about, discuss or pray about the verse that relates most to your life:

Philippians 4:17 Not that I am looking for a gift, but I am looking for what may be credited to your account.

Luke 14:13-14 When you give a banquet, invite the poor, the crippled, the lame, the blind, and you will be blessed. Although they cannot repay you, you will be repaid at the resurrection of the righteous.

Matthew 6:19-21 (Jesus said) "Do not store up for yourselves treasures on earth, where moth and rust destroy, and where thieves break in and steal. But store up for yourselves treasures in heaven, where moth and rust do not destroy, and where thieves do not break in and steal. For where your treasure is, there your heart will be also."

Luke 12:33-34 (Jesus said) " provide purses for yourselves that will not wear out, a treasure in heaven that will not be exhausted, where no thief comes near and no moth destroys. For where your treasure is, there your heart will be also."

Luke 16:9 Use worldly wealth to gain friends for yourselves, so that when it is gone, you will be welcomed into eternal dwellings.

If you ask people what they can "afford to give" to the Lord's work or a special project, they will usually come up with a small amount that they feel they can handle. But if you ask people to determine what God is prompting their heart to give, there is no telling what God will lead them and provide for them to do.

God will often speak a financial amount into a person's heart that is far bigger than their mind can at first grasp. It often takes the mind time to catch up to the amount that God has spoken into a person's heart to give.

Seize the Opportunity

Hundreds of years ago when people mainly lived near the oceans, the word *opportunity* was coined.

It came from the time when ships needed to wait until the tide was in before heading out to sea, otherwise the ship would run aground. In the Latin language, the word "ob portu" described the perfect moment when time and tide converged for a ship to get underway.

Into every person's life come some God-ordained opportunities.

You'll know it's the right time when an urgent, life changing need—something that has eternal and significant value—converges with your ability. At just the right moment, urgency and ability come together. And at that exact moment, you have the opportunity to fulfill a divine purpose God intended for you.

Is it time for you and your congregation to move forward in some special way?

As you reflect back on this 40-day journey you've been on, how is God working in your heart and the lives of others to move out into new waters of faith and service for His glory?

ADAPTED BY PERMISSION OF HARVEST BIBLE CHAPEL
IN ROLLING MEADOWS, IL

IDENTIFY: "WHAT DO YOU FEEL GOD IS CALLING YOU TO DO IN ORDER TO BE MORE GENEROUS TO HIS WORK?"

"God will give you much so that you can give away much, and when we take your gifts to those who need them they will break out into thanksgiving and praise to God for your help." 2 Corinthians 9:11-12

Please review your weekly projects and determine ways God is leading you to live more generously.

Key items/amounts identified in *Week 1* Project (Your income):
1-1: _____ $_____
1-2: _____ $_____
1-3: _____ $_____
1-4: _____ $_____

Key items/amounts identified in *Week 2* Project (Your lifestyle):
2-1: _____ $_____
2-2: _____ $_____
2-3: _____ $_____
2-4: _____ $_____

Key items/amounts identified in *Week 3* Project (Your assets):
3-1: _____ $_____
3-2: _____ $_____
3-3: _____ $_____
3-4: _____ $_____

Key items/amounts identified in *Week 4* Project (Your giving):
4-1: _____ $_____
4-2: _____ $_____
4-3: _____ $_____
4-4: _____ $_____

WHERE WILL YOUR INCREASED GIVING BE GOING?

Which church, special project(s), and/or ministry need(s) do you believe God is leading you to more generously support with the resources you identified on the previous page?

Increased Giving For:

Sources(s) from pg. 73	Amount/Frequency*	Line #
	$　　　／	
	$　　　／	
	$　　　／	
	$　　　／	
	$　　　／	
	$　　　／	
	$　　　／	
	$　　　／	
	$　　　／	

* Frequency: **One-time**, **M:** Monthly, **Q:** Quarterly, **A:** Annually, **P:** Pledge (usually over 1, 2 or 3 years)

What are the reasons you feel it is important to increase your support for the items listed above?

How will this support benefit people for the Lord?

Week 5
SHARING YOUR TREASURES

1. When you started this 40-day journey, were you excited, skeptical, or dreading it? How do you feel now?

2. What is one of the biggest things you've learned about wealth and generosity while going through this journey?

3. What *"lines in the sand"* (pages 65-66) have you crossed in the past? What line in the sand is God calling you to cross now?

4. When you filled out the "Response" worksheet for this week's project, what surprised you or caught your attention in doing this exercise?

5. How do you think this journey will influence your giving to your church? To other ministries? To special needs?

6. What truth or Bible verse from the past seven days of reading stood out to you the most?

7. Have you begun to see God work in your life in fresh ways because of any changes you've begun to make in your finances and giving?

8. Have you experienced any unusual or unexpected financial provisions or blessings in your life since you started this journey? If yes, what have they been?

9. What do you feel God is calling you to do with the opportunity that was introduced in the beginning of this workbook?

10. Can you think of anyone else you know who might benefit from going through this workbook?

Week 6

Do not merely listen to the word, and so deceive yourselves. Do what it says.

James 1:22

DAY 36

When you help the poor and needy don't do it for public recognition.

Think about, discuss or pray about the verse that relates most to your life:

Matthew 6:2-4 (Jesus said) "When you give to the needy, do not announce it with trumpets, as the hypocrites do in the synagogues and on the streets, to be honored by men. I tell you the truth, they have received their reward in full. But when you give to the needy, do not let your left hand know what your right hand is doing, so that your giving may be in secret. Then your Father, who sees what is done in secret, will reward you."

Matthew 23:5-6 (Jesus said) "Everything they do is done for show…they love to sit at the head table at banquets and in the reserved pews in the synagogue!"

Luke 16:15 (Jesus said) "You wear a noble, pious expression in public, but God knows your evil hearts. Your pretense brings you honor from the people, but it is an abomination in the sight of God."

John 5:44 You gladly honor each other, but you don't care about the honor that comes from the only God!

John 12:43 They loved praise from men more than praise from God.

He who bestows his goods upon the poor
shall have as much again, and ten times more.

John Bunyan

Prosperity inebriates men, so that they
take delights in their own merits.

John Calvin

DAY 37

Even your smallest acts of kindness will be remembered and rewarded.

Think about, discuss or pray about the verse that relates most to your life:

Matthew 10:42 Jesus said…"If anyone gives even a cup of cold water to one of these little ones because he is my disciple, I tell you the truth, he will certainly not lose his reward."

Proverbs 19:17 When you help the poor you are lending to the Lord– and he pays wonderful interest on your loan!

Matthew 25:37-40 The righteous will answer him, 'Lord, when did we see you hungry and feed you, or thirsty and give you something to drink? When did we see you a stranger and invite you in, or needing clothes and clothe you? When did we see you sick or in prison and go to visit you?' "The King will reply, 'I tell you the truth, whatever you did for one of the least of these brothers of mine, you did for me.'

Mark 12:41-44 Jesus sat down opposite the place where the offerings were put and watched the crowd putting their money into the temple treasury. Many rich people threw in large amounts. But a poor widow came and put in two very small copper coins, worth only a fraction of a penny. Calling his disciples to him, Jesus said, "I tell you the truth, this poor widow has put more into the treasury than all the others. They all gave out of their wealth; but she, out of her poverty, put in everything– all she had to live on."

*I shovel money out, and God shovels it back…
but God has a bigger shovel!*

Industrialist R. G. LeTourneau

*He is no fool who gives what he cannot keep
to gain what he cannot lose.*

Martyred Missionary Jim Elliot

DAY 38

A main focus for your giving should be your local church & ministry staff.

Think about, discuss or pray about the verse that relates most to your life:

1 Corinthians 9:11-14 If we have sown spiritual seed among you, is it too much if we reap a material harvest from you?…Don't you know that those who work in the temple get their food from the temple, and those who serve at the altar share in what is offered on the altar? In the same way, the Lord has commanded that those who preach the gospel should receive their living from the gospel.

1 Timothy 5:17,18 Pastors who do their work well should be paid well and should be highly appreciated, especially those who work hard at both preaching and teaching. For the Scripture says, "Do not muzzle the ox while it is treading out the grain," and "The worker deserves his wages."

1 Corinthians 9:10 Christian workers should be paid by those they help. Those who do the plowing and threshing should expect some share of the harvest.

Galatians 6:6 Those who are taught the Word of God should help their teachers by paying them.

2 Chronicles 31:9-13 Hezekiah asked the priests about the heaps; the chief priest, answered, "Since the people began to bring their contributions to the temple of the LORD, we have had enough to eat and plenty to spare, because the LORD has blessed his people, and this great amount is left over." They faithfully brought in the contributions, tithes and dedicated gifts.

Deuteronomy 12:19 Be careful not to neglect the Levites (ministers) as long as you live in your land.

*No church ever has a money problem,
only a faithfulness problem.*

Brian Kluth

DAY 39
Building projects are worthy of your support.

Think about, discuss or pray about the verse that relates most to your life:

Exodus 35:29 All the men and women who were willing brought to the LORD freewill offerings for all the work the LORD through Moses had commanded them to do (for the Tabernacle).

1 Chronicles 29:14-16 (David's prayer after people gave generously to a building project) "But who am I, and who are my people, that we should be able to give as generously as this? Everything comes from you, and we have given you only what comes from your hand. We are aliens and strangers in your sight, as were all our forefathers. Our days on earth are like a shadow, without hope. O LORD our God, as for all this abundance that we have provided for building you a temple for your Holy Name, it comes from your hand, and all of it belongs to you."

II Kings 12:7-12 King Joash summoned Jehoiada the priest and the other priests and asked them, "Why aren't you repairing the damage done to the temple?...Jehoiada the priest took a chest and bored a hole in its lid. He placed it beside the altar, on the right side as one enters the temple of the LORD. The priests who guarded the entrance put into the chest all the money that was brought to the temple. Whenever they saw that there was a large amount of money in the chest, the royal secretary and priest came, counted the money that had been brought into the temple of the LORD and put it into bags. When the amount had been determined, they gave the money to the men appointed to supervise the work on the temple. With it they paid those who worked on the temple of the LORD– the carpenters and builders, the masons and stonecutters. They purchased timber and dressed stone for the repair of the temple of the LORD, and met all the other expenses of restoring the temple.

The only investment I ever made which has paid consistently increasing dividends is the money I have given to the Lord.

James Kraft, Founder of Kraft Foods

DAY 40
God will show you other giving opportunities worthy of your support.

Think about, discuss or pray about the verse that relates most to your life:

James 1:27 The Christian who is pure and without fault, from God the Father's point of view, is the one who takes care of orphans and widows, and who remains true to the Lord.

Job 29:12-13 I rescued the poor who cried for help, and the fatherless who had none to assist him. The man who was dying blessed me; I made the widow's heart sing.

Matthew 10:42 And if anyone gives even a cup of cold water to one of these little ones because he is my disciple, I tell you the truth, he will certainly not lose his reward.

Hebrews 13:2-3 Do not forget to entertain strangers, for by so doing some people have entertained angels without knowing it. Remember those in prison as if you were their fellow prisoners, and those who are mistreated as if you yourselves were suffering.

Philippians 4:14 (Paul said to the Christians in Phillipi) You have done right in helping me in my present difficulty.

Acts 28:10 They honored us in many ways and when we were ready to sail, they furnished us with the supplies we needed.

Luke 14:13-14 When you give a banquet, invite the poor, the crippled, the lame, the blind, and you will be blessed. Although they cannot repay you, you will be repaid at the resurrection of the righteous.

You have not lived until you have done something for someone who can never repay you.

John Bunyan 1688

PRACTICAL TIPS FOR GODLY LIFESTYLE ADJUSTMENTS

☑ *Check those that are good reminders for you:*

- Live simply and within your means. *(1 Timothy 6:6-8)*

- Do not covet the possessions of others. *(Ephesians 5:30)*

- Follow this wise advice: "Use it up, wear it out, make it do, or do without."

- When considering making a purchase, ask yourself: "Do I really need this?" Learn to discern between your needs and your wants. *(1 Timothy 6:8-10, Hebrews 13:5)*

- Examine your home for evidence of hoarding. *(Luke 12:18)*

- Give away anything that owns you. *(Matthew 19:21)*

- Do not fall for commercial advertising – shop wisely based on good counsel. *(Proverbs 11:14)*

- Avoid fads; stick with the classics that are always in style. *(Colossians 2:8, Romans 12:1-2)*

- Analyze the cost of seemingly small expenditures, such as eating out, buying brand name clothing, etc. These purchases can add up to substantial sums of money. *(Proverbs 27:23-24)*

- In making major purchases, be sure to shop around, compare prices, gain knowledge, and get at least three prices or bids before making your final decision. *(Proverbs 24:4-5)*

- Actively deaccumulate by going through your closets, drawers, storage spaces, garage, basement, etc. *(Matthew 6:19-20)*

- Be willing to pray before making special purchases. Give God the opportunity to lead you or provide for you in an unexpected but more affordable way. *(1 Peter 5:7)*

- Be willing to purchase or use pre-owned items. Oftentimes you can save substantial money by getting what someone else previously paid full price for. *(Job 27:16, Proverbs 13:22)*

ADAPTED BY PERMISSION OF HARVEST BIBLE CHAPEL
IN ROLLING MEADOWS, IL

Dear Sovereign Lord; Provider and Owner of all I have or ever will have:

I want to thank you for this 40-day journey and the following things you have impressed upon my heart and life that I might live and give more joyfully and generously than ever before:

_____

_____

_____

_____

_____

_____

_____

_____

_____

_____

_____

_____

_____

_____

_____

_____

_____

_____

_____

_____

_____

_____

_____

_____

_____

_____

_____

_____

_____

Signature: _____ Date: _____

If you have been meeting and discussing this devotional booklet with
your spouse, family, group, or class, take time to share highlights of what
you wrote in your letter OR read your letter out loud. Pray together after
everyone has shared.

_P.S. If you would like to send a note about how God used this booklet in your
life, please email Brian Kluth at 40days@kluth.org. THANK YOU!_

Is Your House In Order?
TAKE THIS 10 QUESTION QUIZ TO FIND OUT

Does your spouse, executor, and/or key family members have...

A single document that lists ALL of your financial account numbers, insurance policies, pension, account balances, investments, medical insurance, and important login and password information?	■ YES ■ NO
A single document with the location of your most important personal documents (in most households this is over 30 documents)?	■ YES ■ NO
A single document with your near-the-end-of-your-life medical wishes that your family can provide to medical personnel if you are incapacitated?	■ YES ■ NO
A single document with your detailed funeral wishes?	■ YES ■ NO

A single document indicating who is to receive (or who has been promised) specific family heirlooms and valuable personal possessions?	■ YES ■ NO
A current written will and/or estate plans that honors the Lord by giving a portion of your financial resources to your church and favorite ministries and charities?	■ YES ■ NO
A single document that highlights your life legacy (information about your growing up years, marriage, major turning points, spiritual heritage, and life lessons)?	■ YES ■ NO
All of this information in one booklet and in one place?	■ YES ■ NO
The checklist of 40+ things to do after a loved one dies?	■ YES ■ NO
The biblical insights that helped shape your final decisions?	■ YES ■ NO

IF YOU ANSWERED "NO" TO ANY OF THESE QUESTIONS...

Visit Brian Kluth's website, listen to his sermon message on this subject, and/or consider previewing and ordering the

"CHRISTIAN PLANNING GUIDE FOR GETTING YOUR HOUSE IN ORDER."

In this manual you will find helpful fill-in-the-blank forms and Biblical insights that are available nowhere else. This valuable manual can be ordered and mailed to you OR you can purchase it as an immediately downloadable Microsoft Word document.

To order, go to:
www.kluth.org/houseinorder.htm

GENEROSITY RESOURCES
AND SPEAKING BY BRIAN KLUTH

Rev. Brian Kluth's generosity writing and speaking ministry has stretched across America and to over 100 countries worldwide. Brian is also a Senior pastor in Colorado Springs, Colorado.

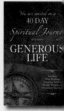

Spiritual Journey to a More Generous Life
Bible Devotional Booklet

This 40 day booklet is being used by churches, denominations, and ministries to inspire greater generosity to the Lord's work.

1-25 copies (**$6.99 each**), *25-50 copies* (**$5.99 each**), *51-100 copies* (**$5.49 ea** *101-199 copies* (**$4.99 each**), *200-500 copies* (**$4.49 each**), *501-1000 copie.* (**$3.99 each**), *1001-2500* copies* (**$3.49 each**), *2501-5000* copies* (**$2.99 ea** *Over 5000 copies* (**Call for a special quote**)
*NOTE ABOUT CUSTOMIZED COPIES: *For orders over 1000 copies, 4 pages of the outs inside booklet covers can be personalized, customized and redesigned for just $1/more per book*

To order, go to:
www.GenerousLife.info or call 1-866-935-5884

If you are calling from outside of the United States, phone: 719-930-4000

Downloadable Generosity Resources For churches and ministries (i.e. PowerPoint offertory slides, generosity pamphlets, committe planning materials, sermon helps, and much more). Go to: **www.kluth.org**

Website Audio & Video Generosity messages, sermons, seminars, and radio broadcasts. Go to: **www.kluth.org/video.htm**

Free Quarterly e-Newsletter On Christian giving for pastors, church leaders, denomination leaders, parachurch ministry leaders, and missionaries. Go to: **www.kluth.org**

Guest Preaching-Teaching at Churches Brian is available for weekend "Generosity Impact Weekends" at churches. Go to: **www.GenerousLife.info** for more information, videos, and available dates

Conference & Seminar Speaker Brian has been a conference speaker or seminar trainer for thousands of pastors and leaders for many denominations, ministerial groups, leadership conferences, conventions, gatherings, and events. For speaking inquiries, email Brian 3-18 months in advance at: **bk@kluth.org**